About t

A native of the Peak District, Simon Mold has spent his working life as a teacher of English and Classics and as a singer in some of England's leading choirs. He has published many articles in well-known musical and literary magazines, and has composed a sizeable body of music which is widely performed. Two albums featuring Simon's music have recently been released: *The Beatific Vision* (on the Herald label), and *Hush, Little Child* (for Heritage), a CD of Christmas carols. A third, that includes a performance of *A Peakland Suite* (pp 93-108), is due for release by Heritage in December 2019.

For my children Dominic, Christopher and Alexander

Simon Mold

POETRY OF THE PEAK

with illustrations by

DAVID BOTHAM

AUSTIN MACAULEY PUBLISHERS™

LONDON * CAMBRIDGE * NEW YORK * SHARJAH

A CIP catalogue record for this title is available from the British Library.

ISBN 9781528930376 (Paperback)
ISBN 9781528966269 (ePub e-book)

www.austinmacauley.com

First Published (2019)
Austin Macauley Publishers Ltd
25 Canada Square
Canary Wharf
London
E14 5LQ

Cover photo: Mam Tor in the Peak District

Acknowledgements

I wish to record my great appreciation of David Botham's company, encouragement, photography and artistic skills in connection with *Poetry of the Peak*. All illustrations, and the reproduction of the painting on page 81, are © David Botham. Photographs are all © Simon Mold and David Botham, apart from those on pages 85 and 88/89 which are © Peter Fox and Hulleys of Baslow respectively, to whom I offer my thanks. Additional thanks are also due to Richard Eades (Hulleys of Baslow), Alison Fox (Longnor Craft Centre & Coffee Shop) and Bob Smail (New House Farm, Kniveton). I am also grateful to Vinh Tran at Austin Macauley for his help, advice and expertise, and to Dr Roger Scoppie for his proof-reading assistance.

Finally I should like to offer my gratitude to Ian McMillan, Ian Green, Lizzie Ballagher, Amanda Fitchett and other friendly folk who have provided encouragement and helpful comments along the way; and ultimately to everyone, from my parents onward, who has enabled me to enjoy and appreciate the Peak District's special charms.

Simon Mold
October 2019

Contents

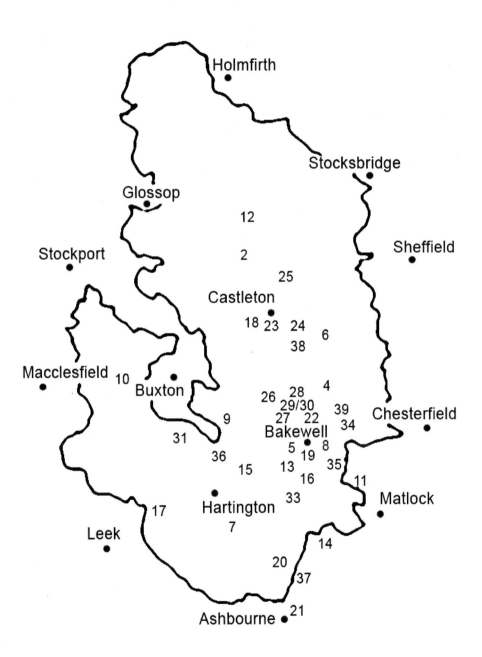

The Peak District showing the National Park boundary

Holmfirth

Stocksbridge

Glossop

Stockport

Sheffield

12

2

25

Castleton

18 23 24

6

38

Macclesfield 10

Buxton

26 28

4

29/30

39

27 22

34

Chesterfield

9

Bakewell

31

5 8

36

19

15 13 35

16 11

Hartington 33

Matlock

17

7

Leek

14

20

37

Ashbourne 21

(Numbers indicate a poem's locale)

Author's Preface

The hills and dales of north Derbyshire and parts of neighbouring counties were already being called Peakland over a thousand years ago by the Anglo-Saxons. Six hundred years ago the region was dubbed a Wonder, and by the early 1600s the Peak boasted seven 'official' Wonders of its own that pioneering and rather intrepid travellers came in person to experience. Since then all sorts of other aspects of this Wonderful district have gradually, and quite rightly in this writer's view, come to be so recognised; perhaps some of them featured in the poetry of William Newton (1750-1830), the so-called Minstrel of the Peak, except that we shall never know since his writings are virtually all lost.

I therefore offer this collection as my small attempt at saluting within the pages of a single volume some of the things I feel a latter-day Peakland Minstrel ought by rights to be singing about, with the emphasis on those special places and features of the landscape that he senses will reward the traveller of today. All the poems will moreover be found to be written in verse of one kind or another, including some metrical forms common in William Newton's time and which he surely used himself. With luck something in the following pages will encourage further exploration of one of England's loveliest and most striking rural regions – the Peak District.

Simon Mold
October 2019

1. The Seven Wonders Of The Peak

All the Peak's a thrill,
And all its hills and valleys quite enchanting,
They have their champions, and their devotees,
But poets once extolled especial sights
They dubbed The Seven Wonders. First, **Poole's Cavern**,
Tourist-trap since eighteen-fifty-three;
And then a **Well** at Tideswell, which was thought
To ebb and flow according to the tide
Of oceans far away. And then **Mam Tor**,
Whose surface slides and shivers, though they say
Its shadow stays the same. Then **Eldon Hole**,
A hundred-foot-deep chasm in the rock,
Wide, steep and black, that was held bottomless,
And plumbed, according to the finest minds,
The centre of the earth. And then the **Well**
In stately Buxton, sacred to St Anne
(And to a local goddess long before)
Whose crystal waters wooed the sick and lame,
And soothed their aches and pains. Another Wonder
Takes us back to hilly Castleton,
And to (excuse my French) the Devil's Arse –
Peak Cavern, if we need to be polite,
Which boasts the greatest cavemouth in the land,
And glistening stygian waters that enthralled
A shepherd long ago. The last delight
That ends the Seven Wonders of our tale
Is **Chatsworth**, Palace of the Peak, suffused
With grace, with style, with taste – with everything.

(Cf As You Like It, II vii)

Over Hill, Over Dale

2. Jacob's Ladder

I first climbed Jacob's Ladder at the age of 43 –
"Walker's Honour", so you know I'm not pretending,
I say this now for those of you who don't like tragedy
(So you know my story has a happy ending).
I parked the car at Edale and set off along the track,
And the ground at first was fairly easy going,
The sun was barely shining through a mat of cloudy black,
But at least, I thought, it hasn't started snowing.
The dale appeared quite eerie underneath its heavy air,
And the constant birdless silence was unnerving,
But the height of Kinder beckoned me, atop its stony stair,
So I followed with no further thought of swerving.
Then "Cuckoo" caught my ear; and then I heard a second cry:
I scanned the valley, searching for the caller,
Then there it was…and in a flash the bird had passed me by
And was on its way to Kinder, ever smaller.
A while or more of slogging, and I'd come to Barber Booth,
A lonely, stony outpost built for cattle,
And thence the journey underfoot was markedly less smooth,
A presage of my hard forthcoming battle.
You come at last upon a pretty bridge that spans the stream,
And there I sat, remembering the story
Of Jacob in the desert, and the angels in his dream
Who climbed up on a ladder high to glory.
Well, I was not an angel, but uphill I had to go,
So with bold and cheerful heart began ascending,
My body quickly told me that the journey would be slow,
For the steps above were steep and never-ending.
My breath soon came in rushes, and I couldn't keep the pace,
While my toiling limbs together groaned and grumbled,
My agony and anguish must have shown upon my face
As I grimly, ever upwards, gasped and stumbled.
Finally, half-crawling, I had made it to the top
Where I gratefully collapsed, my heart a-pounding,
I almost cursed the mountain that had almost made me drop,
But for awe at vistas endless and astounding.
So there I stood, the momentary lord of my redoubt,
The victor-victim of my pain and pleasure:
Aloft upon the plateau of majestic Kinder Scout,
I had found what no philosopher could measure.

3. Waters Of The Peak

I love these Peakland streams that flow
In pebbly bed or verdant vale,
Where drifts of water avens blow,
And dippers dive in Longdendale:
By tinkling weir and timeless mill
The well-dressed waters chatter still.

The peaty torrents of the tors
Join hands to dance across a bluff
Whence thund'rous Kinder Downfall pours
To clatter in its lonely clough;
And Grindsbrook winds away below
To tease the tide of rippling Noe.

In Wye's wide meads I'd spend my days
And gaze on Monsal Head above,
By Lathkill's limpid rill I'd laze,
Or tread the stones o'er tumbling Dove,
While tawny trout flash by my feet
To make an angler's day "compleat".

But where I crave the noblest scene
The stately Derwent slips in style
From Ladybower's lakeland sheen
To Chatsworth's grand palatial pile:
Sweet waters! Runes in nature's rhyme,
And gossips till the end of time.

Lathkill Dale

4. Millstone Grit

By Peakland paths, above her snaky dales
The pilgrim climbs, by birch or thorny whin;
Atop such slopes grim rugged ridges grin,
And nurse dark tales.

Belike, with leering sneer, an age ago
Some Tempter in this wilderness once said,
Man, turn the very bedrock into bread!
And it was so.

And thus he bent to labour, brave and bold
And prised great stones from Curbar's ancient Edge,
With axe and hammer, pick, and rope, and wedge,
For mills of old.

What famines did these stones keep from the door?
Which thousands of our forebears did they feed?
How many ears were ground, so dames could knead
The dough of yore?

Now, scattered and abandoned, grindstones lie.
Like wheels from carriages long since decayed
They cluster close, hard by the rocky shade
Of quarried wall,

As if, two hundred years ago, a score
Of hewing hands downed tools one day, but then
Came sudden, knelling news; so toiling men
Trudged back no more.

Today, as twilight's embers disappear,
And curious mortals leave these lonely knolls,
Perhaps they sense the spirits of those souls
Who once slaved here.

5. Lathkill Dale

Fair flows the Lathkill through her sweet ravine,
Half-hiding within ash-clad, steepling hills,
Her waters clear as glass, the queen of rills,
Her fishy pools reflectent and serene.

What past endeavours have her waters seen?
The miners dug here once, and strove for lead
That kept a roof of sorts, and bought their bread
Until her freshets washed their workings clean.

Now Jacob's ladder graces ancient spoil
And orchids bloom untroubled in the grass
Oft-hidden from our unsuspecting gaze,

While she, no longer witness to sad toil
Drifts onward down her dale, as strollers pass
By Conksbury Bridge, where currents loll and laze.

6. Carl Wark

Up through Padley, on the top
By Burbage Moor
There rests, aloof, a fighting ship
Long beached ashore,
With rocky hull and once proud prow –
But where are all its crewmen now?

In summer, on a glittering day
The walkers come
To scrape and scramble up its slopes
That seem less glum
When sunrays make the old rocks grin
Like drinkers at the Fox House Inn.

Yet when the mists are mizzling, then
Half-peers a hulk:
Dry-docked atop a peaty sea
It seems to sulk;
Stove in, like Noah's battered hat,
On Peakland's private Ararat.

7. Piscatoribus Sacrum

When Izaak met Charles in a bend of the Dove
The sun fluttered down through the mantle above,
The mist lingered longer, but up went the cry,
"'Tis a morn, my good friend, for the cast of a fly!"

On precipitous bank could the pair barely roam,
Leaving stepping-stones washed by each fleck of white foam;
As the sun wiped the night from his glistening eye –
"Where best," came the call, "for the cast of a fly?"

By the Twelve stern Apostles the twain lightly trod
Then Tissington Spires gave the champions their nod;
On and on past the cave of one wily and sly:
"Shall Reynard begrudge us the cast of a fly?"

As the light hovered bright over Pickering Tor
The pair turned their gaze to the westernmost shore
Where Ilam's tall Rock towered into the sky –
"Few leagues now, my friend, till the cast of a fly!"

With the stream brave with kingcups and cloudy with midge
Two votaries strode over Viator's Bridge
To a fane, and a fire, and an ale, and plum pie,
"And the finest of seats for the cast of our fly!"

Dovedale

The Latin motto Piscatoribus Sacrum – *'Sacred to Fishermen' – can be found carved above the door of the 'fishing temple' built by Charles Cotton (1630-1687) for himself and his friend Izaak Walton (1593-1683) on the banks of the River Dove in Beresford Dale. The pair helped popularise the sport of angling, with Walton achieving literary immortality following the publication of his famous book "The Compleat Angler" in 1653. Various natural features along the stretch of the river upstream from the stepping stones beneath Thorpe Cloud bear fanciful names such as Reynard's Cave and Tissington Spires. Viator's Bridge over the Dove at Milldale is named after Viator ('The traveller') in* The Compleat Angler, *who engages in informative discourses with his friend and mentor Piscator ('The fisherman').*

Charles and Izaak's 'fishing temple'

8. In Calton Pastures

So we set off, just she and I,
Past the Outrake, then up high
Where golfers' balls come dribbling by,
To Wicksop Wood.

In, still we slogged it, left and right
Until a teasing shaft of light
Announced that we had gained the height
Where now we stood.

So then, up steps and over stile,
We panted, puffed, then paused awhile
And turned, and drank in mile on mile
Of upland wine.

Then, with what breath we still possessed
We turned our gaze toward the west,
Until I murmured a request:
Will you be mine?

Then time itself was breathless there,
As skylarks skirled through hazy air,
And breezes riffled through her hair
Which rose and fell;

In Calton Pastures did we lie,
Our gazes supping on the sky,
Until she answered, by and by.
And hearts breathed well.

Roads Well Travelled

9. The Street

"*Aquae Arnametiae.*"
"We'll go there then," the corps commander said.
"We'll dam the spring, and line the sides with lead.
We'll need a road."

At *Lutudarum*
The usual suspects weren't in any doubt
(That is to say, the farmers round about
They commandeered).

Via Plumbea?
(That's just a guess; what Romans called The Street
That was to echo with their tramping feet
We'll never know,)

But, *ex nihilo*
A road was born: sods dug, long straights surveyed,
Stone hewed, transported, tamped, until they'd laid
A hill-borne way.

In illo tempore
Did any Caesar ever come to know
The way from Wirksworth, north by Minninglow
To Buxton's springs?

Peregrinantes -
Did man and beast bring treasures of the mine
To cast into their ancient forebears' shrine
And pray for bread?

Nunc ubi est?
Part washed away, part hidden, part 'alive'
Beneath a modern route (A515)
That keeps its course,

Straight, more or less,
With odd concessions, just a kink or two
That surely proves this saying to be true:
In via veritas.

Roman roads were called streets because in Latin they were stratae, *i.e. bestrewn (with metalling), or paved. If there was only one local Roman road then it would just have been The Street. The evidence of the Roman road from Buxton to Derby is certain until it peters out below Minninglow Hill: where had it come from? Very possibly Wirksworth, as the Wirksworth Archaeological Society persuasively argues (at* **www.wirksworthromanproject.co.uk***). Wirksworth was conceivably the location of Lutudarum, a name that is found stamped on pigs of Roman lead. The Roman road network in the Peak District has been underestimated for many years, and there's still room for additional and literally ground-breaking research.*

Aquae Arnametiae – Buxton
Lutudarum – Wirksworth (?)
Via Plumbea – The Leaden Way
Ex nihilo – Out of nothing
In illo tempore – At that time
Peregrinantes – Wayfaring
Nunc ubi est? – Where is it now?
In via veritas – Truth is to be found upon the highway

The Street (A515)

10. A Motorist's Nursery Rhyme

The old *Cat and Fiddle*
Stands bang in the middle
Of moorland that's rugged and steep,
It's surrounded by masses
Of tussocky grasses
And hundreds of lubberly sheep.

Though views can be glorious,
The road is notorious
With savants aware of the trends,
As hordes of swift bikers
Outnumber the hikers,
And hellishly hare round the bends.

It's dreadfully twisty,
Inclined to be misty,
And rarely is fog a surprise,
And if you are straining
To see when it's raining,
Such speed is not awfully wise.

The inn's situation
And high elevation
Both make it seem rather remote,
But since 1813
This hostelry's been
A familiar landmark of note.

So, if you are driving
And patiently striving
To combat the fog or the snow,
The pub's a delight
On a dark, stormy night...
Though there's six goddam miles still to go!

Reputedly England's second-highest hostelry, the Cat and Fiddle *Inn stands halfway along the notoriously tortuous road between Buxton and Macclesfield, to which it has lent its name and which is regularly beset with extreme weather conditions, slow lorries and bikers in a hurry – a challenging combination. On a good day (there are some), views can be spectacular, but it's best to concentrate on negotiating the next bend, especially given the additional hazard of suicidal sheep that can't apparently tell the difference between grass and tarmac. This route is supposed to be a quicker way to and from the M6, avoiding Stockport. Everything's relative…*

The Cat and Fiddle: a wild and woolly landscape

11. Get Your Kicks...

London – Glasgow – Inverness – Thurso:
South to north on the old A6,
Conjuring scenes of Peakland pleasures
The road still holds a bag of tricks.

Matlock where they took the waters,
Hydros, hills and healing springs,
Up and on to a Dale called Darley
Where the Whitworths' name still rings.

Then to Rowsley of the railway
Where great sidings used to be,
Smoke, and shunt, and clash and clatter,
Silent now 'neath thorn and tree.

Over Derwent by "The Peacock",
Then a mill that grinds away,
Soon to reach the Hall of Haddon,
Where romantic legends play.

Haddon Fields and Burton Closes
(Gothic pile from Paxton's page),
Into Bakewell of the Pudding,
Bones and stones of bygone age.

Up to Ashford-in-the-Water
With its pretty Sheepwash Bridge,
Duke's Drive leads to Ashwood Dale
Where snows can lie from road to ridge.

Winding up towards the plateau
Where the road splits into two,
Taddington now free of traffic
(How of yore did trucks get through?)

Down, with vistas panoramic,
Round the spur of Topley Pike
Views of railway, limestone quarry,
Monsal Trail for boot and bike.

Then it's bends, all twisty-turny
As we track the Wye upstream,
Underneath the railway arches,
Stony loads and ghosts of steam.

Matlock – Rowsley – Bakewell– Buxton:
Peakland's path from spa to spa –
Park by Crescent, sip from flask…then
Pat obliging motorcar!

12. No Through Road

The breeze has dropped by Doctor's Gate,
The car lights zigzag to and fro,
And slopes of steepling hills await
The all-implicit fall of snow;

The sky's become that curious hue,
A yellow-brown that presses hard
And warns of wintery weather due
To wearied drivers off their guard;

And now the flakes begin to curl,
And kiss the road with melting lips,
Until each fleckling starts to swirl,
And finds a purchase, sticks, and grips;

As inn lights beckon in the mind
And Glossop seems so far away,
Surrendering windscreens shape to blind
Each driver trapped by gloam and grey;

And now the wind, that first feigned sleep
Jumps like a sprung jack-in-a box,
To cut a caper, skip, and leap
In frenzy over road and rocks;

As smothering snow lays flesh on bones
The Snake Pass sighs, yields up its ghost,
While drivers tap on furious phones
And message those they love the most.

A night... a morning, drear and dense...
Within each bubble of a car,
A toil of travellers shivers, tense,
Awaiting succour from afar.

13. Paradox In The White Peak

Abroad on one of Peakland's twisting lanes
I'm stuck behind a grinding, growly lorry,
While on the verges dusty, snowy stains
Betray white lime coaxed daily from the quarry.

As both of us attack another bend
And reach a heady twenty miles an hour,
And poisoned, pumping fuel emissions send
A toxic puss through wayside tree and flower,

I ponder, nonetheless, the nation's need
For stone, and lime, and products of the land
That nestle under mountain, moss or mead –
A crux we sometimes strain to understand,

Whereby the fruits of each defacing scar
Sustain each road that bears the tourist's car.

14. The *Via Gellia* – A Handy Guide

The way from Cromford to Grangemill
Was named the *Via Gellia*
At some point in the eighteenth cent.
By P. E. Gell, a local gent
Of Roman (so he claimed) descent –
A jolly decent felliah.

Well, how to say the *Via* word:
No need to fret – I'll tellia –
Though "wee-ah" was J. Caesar's way,
It tends to rhyme with "choir" today,
And makes it easier to say
If you're a local dwellia.

I have another helpful hint
To aid the weaker spellia:
The *V* is like the *v* in *vine*,
And not the *w* in *wine*
That P. E. drank, so rare and fine,
And laid down in his cellia.

And as for Gell, whose name became
The Latin-sounding *Gellia* –
The *G*'s a *J*, as found in *joke* –
He was an enterprising bloke,
Whose kinsmen lived as gentlefolk:
Well-off, like Rockefellia.

Now, if to stray along "Gells' Way"
An impulse should impellia,
Beware! – for from each verdant tree
The raindrops drip down constantly –
(Which makes the ground more slippery,
And jellia, and smellia…)

So take a large umbrellia!

Supernatural Solicitings

15. Arbor Low

Drear broods the crow by Arbor Low;

          For why?

Does she bewray
In some strange way
The sobs these stones would sigh?
If only they would try!

What runes were spelled, what moots were held;

          What rites?

If dust could sing,
This ancient ring
Would echo on these heights
To strains of grim delights.

Through mist-filled air each stony stare

          Ill-met

Outglares my gaze
Which jibs and strays;
While mute, with wings of jet
The cruel crow lingers yet.

Arbor Low ("Earthwork Hill") is the Peak District's premier stone circle, and although it has been dubbed "The Stonehenge of the North" it is known by far fewer people than its Wiltshire contemporary. Maybe its upland, windswept and rather inaccessible location has helped it keep its secrets. Perhaps 4000 years old, it must have been a major religious centre. "Low" is from the Old English hlaw, *meaning hill, and is nothing to do with the adjective "low", which is of Norse origin. A Peak District low thus tends to be rather high. These days sheep nibble the nearby grass, but in Neolithic times any animal that got this close in search of a succulent lunch probably ran the risk of ending up on the sacrificial altar. Or so the local crows doubtless hoped.*

16. Nine Ladies Dancing

A merchant rich had daughters nine
(Live happy, quoth the Devil),
The merchant loved his daughters nine,
And fed them well on meat and wine –
Too well! bethought the Devil.

Their beauty bloomed, these daughters nine
(Live happy, quoth the Devil),
So handsome were these daughters nine
No other maids were thought so fine –
Aha! bethought the Devil.

The merchant upped, one April day
(Live happy, quoth the Devil),
The merchant said, that April day,
He must to foreign climes away –
'Tis well! bethought the Devil.

Now be ye godly, daughters fair
(Live happy, quoth the Devil),
Stay pure and sinless, daughters fair
While I must needs breathe salty air –
Fair wind! bethought the Devil.

Now, while their sire was far away
(Live happy, quoth the Devil),
They sighed that he was far away,
But laughed when dawned the first of May –
Sweet morn! bethought the Devil.

A wandering fiddler came to town
(Live happy, quoth the Devil),
The fiddler played about the town
And each fair daughter donned her gown –
How fine! bethought the Devil.

Out passed the damsels through their door
(Live happy, quoth the Devil),
The fiddler led them from their door
Up and away to Stanton Moor –
Well met! bethought the Devil.

And there they danced, and he did play
(Live happy, quoth the Devil),
The dance grew quick as he did play
Although 'twas now the Sabbath Day –
Not long! bethought the Devil.

Then as the whipping wind made moan –
(Live happy, quoth the Devil),
A fearful, ghastly, hellish moan,
Each figure froze…and turned to stone –
They're mine! rejoiced the Devil.

*

'Tis said, upon a stormy night
(Live happy, quoth the Devil),
Within the ring, as black as night
A figure dances in delight –
'Tis I! exults the Devil.

Stanton Moor near Birchover, high above the River Derwent, is home to an assorted array of cairns and stones, including the ring of Nine Ladies who of course were once beautiful maidens who sinfully danced on the Sabbath to the strains of a lone fiddler. The latter, in the shape of the King's Stone about 100 feet away, suffered the same eternal petrification as the dancers, although he is claimed to come to life once a year to reprise his set. Whether the Devil had anything to do with their collective punishment is technically uncertain, but it does seem to be the kind of weekend dampener that Old Nick might well have been happy to claim for his CV.

17. Mermaid

Within dank waters drear I dwell,
Where few lights play,
Though what I think of this my hell
Is hard to say.
Am I content?
Or do I pine
For tresses gold, and long, which once were mine?

No bird disturbs my watery roof
With cheerful flight,
No swishing tail, no cloven hoof
Strays into sight.
Am I still fair?
No man may know
Except he brave the devilish dark below.

Yet as, unloved, a clawing troll,
My heart unstilled,
I watch beside the silent soul
Of him I killed,
I know but this:
No ghost, or fool
Will wed the weeping witch of Black Mere Pool.

A small body of water near Leek called Black Mere Pool aka Blake Meer or indeed Blakemere Pond, from which no livestock will drink and over which no bird will fly, is said to be haunted by a demon mermaid, clearly a near-relative of Grendel's mother. According to one explanation a certain Joshua Linnet was once rejected by a girl to whom he had made advances, so promptly had her condemned as a witch and drowned in the Pool. However, her final utterance was a deadly curse, which was clearly most effective since Joshua was discovered lying lifeless by the water's edge three days later, his face scarred with claw marks. Moral: cut a witch's tongue out as a precaution before drowning her.

18. Incident At Winnats Pass

"Let's walk up through Winnats," said Clara one day –
"The mutts could both do with an outing."
So the newly-weds parked and set off on their way
Amidst barks and occasional shouting.
As the two King Charles spaniels sniffed into the air
Young Clara held Allan's hand tightly,
When they reached the east side of the Shivering Hill
And stood, by the fork, momentarily still,
And the dogs gave a whine, as if sensing a chill,
"Oh, it's nothing!" their mistress laughed lightly.

So they walked up the Pass flanked by acres of green
That rose on each side ever higher,
The dogs were excited, and pulling, and keen:
Henrietta and daughter Maria.
Then on a dark bend, with the sun sinking low,
Where the hills hemmed them in without quarter,
Both animals stopped, with a jerk, by a rock:
The mother yowled shrilly, and backed, as in shock,
And then it was seconds too late to take stock
As Clara let go of the daughter.

Off bounded Maria as fast as a rabbit,
Her lead behind dusty and trailing,
And after her Clara bent down hard to grab it
But tripped on a stone and went flailing.
How awkward her landing was Allan could tell,
As in pain her blue eyes slowly misted,
So, pursuing Maria before she could flee
Then securing the dogs by the bough of a tree,
He comforted Clara, whose ankle and knee
Were quite bloody, and swollen, and twisted.

She gritted her teeth in the teeth of the pain,
And her last drops of tea were a blessing,
As the sun left the sky and it spotted with rain,
Alan searched for an improvised dressing.
A handkerchief served; then he searched for their phones,
But after ten minutes of trying,
Both signals were dead, wheresoever he strode;
So they pondered, and looked left and right up the road,
Till an old battered van came towards them, and slowed,
And drew up near to where she was lying.

Her husband went up to the driver, who spoke:
"Th'ad better look sharp, lad, and fetch 'er."
In relief Allan nodded and managed to joke
That they'd "somehow forgotten a stretcher!"
Half carried, half hobbled, through rusty back doors
The patient sank down on the seating:
Above were some picks and cloth caps on a rack,
And candlewax half-falling out of a sack;
But three indistinct forms also crouched in the back
'Mid the shadows, and offered no greeting.

The dogs were untied, and they boarded the van
With their master, all shoving and squeezing,
With darkness fast falling their ordeal began
With the old motor coughing and wheezing.
"Tha mun have a sup for thi sen" came a growl,
So the girl reached and quaffed, with a shudder,
The flask passed to Allan, who also drank deep,
And the wind howled without as the pair fought off sleep
Till they slumped on their seat in a stupefied heap,
And the van came to rest with a judder.

It took a few days to unleash an alarm
When the group showed no signs of returning,
The fear that they'd come to some terrible harm
Was acute, and perplexing, and burning.
But in spite of appeals and the searchers dispatched,
Bit by bit expectations were banished
As folk by their fireside, or snug in their beds
Concluded, along with the wisest old heads
That two pedigree pets, and two young newly-weds
Had walked off through the Pass…and just vanished.

In an old local hostelry, many months on,
A hiker, a-tremble, was speaking:
"I was walking down Winnats, at dusk, whereupon
A cold wind started wailing and shrieking;
A van driver gave me a sharp, chilling stare –
Then drove on while the gale became stronger,
All at once, quite unseen, a man uttered a cry,
And a woman screamed out as if like for to die,
And the hill seemed to shake, and there came a great sigh –
Then all ceased; and the wind blew no longer."

When the longstanding landlady learned what he'd said,
She was filled with unease and misgiving:
Long ago in the Pass murdered roamers had bled,
And the dead still called out to the living.
"Let a man dig down deep by the old engine shaft,
And be mindful of ought he discovers."
So a team ventured forth to a low earthen mound,
And, to tell the tale shortly, the gravediggers found
Two skeletal dogs lying there in the ground
And the bones of two young wedded lovers.

The remains were reburied with obsequies due,
And Castleton mourned, as was fitting,
When the hiker returned to the inn, where a few
Of the regulars spotted him sitting.
The fire in the van driver's eyes, he declared,
Was so hellish he couldn't forget him;
The landlady whispered: "The van that you saw
Was crushed years ago in a crash that killed four –
But the driver drives on as a ghost, evermore:
He'd been many moons dead when you met him."

A Derbyshire legend that has been around for over two hundred years has it that two well-heeled eighteenth-century lovers, traditionally named Allan and Clara, were murdered in remote Winnats Pass by a group of lead miners, who initially escaped justice but who each, one by one, came to a sticky end. The lovers' skeletons were said to have been discovered buried in a sack, and were afterwards reburied in Castleton churchyard. History fails to record whether or not they were additionally the owners of two King Charles Spaniels…

Custom and Practice

Bakewell Pudding

19. A Pudding Is Born

"Mrs Greaves, Mrs Greaves, I'm so sorry, I am,
And I know that you want to know why
I poured all the egg mixture onto the jam,"
Wept the pastry cook, wiping her eye.

"When you gave me instructions for making your tart,
My mind was elsewhere," she confessed.
But her mistress rejoined, "Dry your tear, cheer your heart –
For I bring you acclaim from our guest:

"He had ordered a tart; but a mouthful he took,
And approval was swiftly displayed –
So he asked me to say to my wonderful cook
That a wonderful pudding she'd made!"

"But into the pastry," the cook said, bemused,
"The egg mixture should have been stirred.
I admit my mistake, but I was quite confused
When you told me, and must have misheard."

Then replied Mrs Greaves: "You have no need to fret:
To your skill we must all raise a cap.
And as for your pudding, I'll make a small bet
That it could put our town on the map!"

The Bakewell Pudding is usually said to have originated in the nineteenth century when, whilst making a strawberry tart, a cook at the Rutland Arms Inn mistakenly poured some egg mixture over the strawberry jam instead of stirring it into the pastry. The result of this accident was a hit with some influential diners and, naturally, with the proprietor Mrs Greaves (Sir Joseph Paxton's sister-in-law, incidentally) who encouraged the cook to continue to produce her new local delicacy. Although the recipe was thenceforward jealously guarded, rival purveyors of Bakewell Puddings trade locally to this day. Any visitor who is unfortunate enough to refer to the said confectionery as a "tart" may, however, be extremely lucky to survive the experience…

20. Children's Well-Dressing Song

We dress the wells in Derbyshire,
Come spring or summer days,
With blooms, and bark, and grown things
From woods and country ways.
Their waters flow from year to year
Though fields be dead and dry,
And so we children dress the wells –
Sophia, Tom and I.

For weeks the wooden trays are soaked
Before they lay them down,
And then we knead the clammy clay
Until it's beaver-brown,
We paw it and we pummel it
With never fear or fuss,
As Mum finds it amusing when
It goes all over us…

And then we're off to comb the lanes
For mosses, cones and flowers,
(Which keeps us off computer screens,
And occupied for hours).
To owners of large gardens
We're especially polite,
In case we need to raid them
In the middle of the night.

We spread the clay upon a board
Until it's nice and flat,
And now the paper drawing's brought
And laid on top of that.
We blackknob all the outlines,
To make them bold and dark
With alder cones, or hogweed,
Or rhubarb seeds, or bark.

At last it's time for petalling,
With thousands to be done,
Like overlapping roof slates –
The marathon's begun!
With all that bending over
Your poor back begins to ache,
And then you think you've finished…
Till you notice a mistake.

But finally the picture's done,
And all can breathe a sigh,
And out it's taken to the well,
Exposed to sun and sky.
Standing proud for all to see
It weathers rain or shine,
And proudly we walk up, and point,
And say, "That petal's mine!"

And after all the dressing
When the flowers look their best,
We give our thanks for water,
And the village wells are blessed.
We lap up all the compliments –
Despite the constant danger
That Mrs Brown might stop, and think
"Is that my prize hydrangea?"

The practice of decorating wells and springs with flowers is an especially endearing Derbyshire custom that dates from time immemorial. The ceremonies at Tissington were for many years the best known, whilst nowadays wells are dressed during spring and summer all over the Peak District, with the emphasis on communal participation that of course includes the local children. Traditional designs use only the produce of the natural world, and the decorating process is painstaking and skilled. Biblical scenes are usually popular, although designs can encompass all manner of country topics or subjects that have a particular local significance.

21. The Beautiful Game

If yer Up'ard or Down'ard it don't matter which
Cos yer bound to get muddy or fall in a ditch,
If yuv come when we're playin', yer'll know that yuv been
Since it's mayhem round here after *God Save The Queen*.

Some fancy celeb comes to turn up the ball,
And then yer like bricks in some mad human wall –
Round the town, in the brook, in a giant-sized hug,
Yer can't keep away once yuv caught this mad bug.

No murderin', no maimin'; but that's not to say
Yer can't politely shove other folk out the way –
And when the ball's goaled, you can cheer with delight,
For yer pancakes'll taste all the better that night!

The Ashbourne Shrovetide Football Match is played annually on Shrove Tuesday and Ash Wednesday. "Football" and "played" are relative terms. There is a ball, but spectators sight it infrequently as it is for long periods concealed within the steaming hug of participants. After the playing of the National Anthem, two teams of young men, the Up'ards and Down'ards depending on which part of the town they reside in, attempt to manoeuvre the ball towards opposing goals situated three miles apart. Occasionally they succeed. Crowds keep a respectful distance. The St John Ambulance is on hand. Tactics are not overly subtle; even the 1970s Leeds Utd squad would have appeared elfinly sylph-like by comparison. The event is entirely and utterly off the wall, yet brilliantly British, barmy and Brexit-proof.

Likely Stories

22. A Capricious Tale

A farmer up at Parsley Hay
Had several goats to sell one day,
So asked his friend to take them down
To market, in fair Bakewell town.
And so his friend, Teetotal Stan,
Hitched a trailer to his van,
And when he'd got the goats inside
He took them on the eight-mile ride
To Bakewell, where he'd have a bite
To eat, and sojourn overnight,
And move the van next morning, park it,
Then take all the goats to market.

Now, it must be said that Stan
Was not a conscientious man,
And, what is more, his soubriquet
Ironic was in every way,
Because all knew he'd never snub
A chance to shelter in the pub,
And see his glass was rarely dry
While all the world just passed him by.
And so 'twas on this Sunday that
He gave the goats a friendly pat,
Then left the van without a care
And set off for the market square
To find an alehouse, ever blest,
Where Stan would spend his Day of Rest.

When midnight struck, and Stan was tight,
They thrust him out into the night;
He lurched, as only drunkards can,
Back to where he'd left the van
And, with a final sozzled leap,
Flopped inside, and fell asleep,
To snore the darkling night away
Right through until the break of day.

Now, gentle Reader, 'tis the time
When tragedy o'ertakes my rhyme:
For, though the trailer gate was shut,
Its fastener bore a loosened nut
Which made security less clean
Than otherwise it might have been;
And yet, when Stan had walked away,
He'd left his goats with nought but hay,
So that, with deepening disquiet,
They sought to supplement their diet.

And so, while Stan, with snort and snore
Was sleeping off the night before,
His hungry cargo kicked the gate
Which started to disintegrate:
The catch broke off – and with great glee
And one swift bound the goats were free.

Next morning, when the sun's first rays
Inspired the birds to fulsome praise,
Teetotal Stan awoke once more,
And, though to start with not quite sure
Whose vehicle he was in, or why,
He watched the sun climb in the sky,
And then considered his position,
Remembering his market mission;
So, stepping gingerly outside,
With eyes still hardly open wide,
He groped his way along the wall
To give the goats their morning call.
Imagine, Reader, the surprise

That greeted Stan's astonished eyes:
The damaged wood, the broken latch,
The open gate without its catch;
But, worst of all, to Stan's distress:
A total, utter… goatlessness.

Some hours before Stan's worried frown,
The goats had fanned out through the town,
Embarking on a spree of crime
That would re-echo down through time.
Bath Gardens were the first to know
How feared a goat is as a foe:
At 5 a.m. one trotted through
The gate, and stopped, surveyed the view,
Scanned with delight the flowery beds,
Then promptly tore the blooms to shreds.
Dahlias, nasturtiums too,
Marigolds, aubretia blue –
All proceeded down the throat
Of one intensely hungry goat,
For every corner brimmed with flowers
That kept the gourmet glad for hours…

Another famished goat, meanwhile
Desired to breakfast in some style,
So when she took her morning sniff,
To her delight she caught a whiff
Of lettuce, carrots, apples, pears,
As marketeers laid out their wares.
So, following this heady scent,

Trip, trap across the bridge she went
(A bridge devoid of any troll
Who might have checked her ravening stroll).
Unchallenged, then, by man or beast,
This second goat eyed up her feast,
While traders chatted, cruelly blind
To what grim Fortune had in mind.
First, anything remotely green
As fitting for *hors d'oeuvres* was seen,
Nor did our quadruped forget
To sample sprout, or fat courgette,
And thereby cause intense dismay
Because she didn't stop and pay.

At length a desperate hue and cry
Was raised by startled passers-by,
But by this time our goat was wise
To every ruse or lame surprise,
And each stallholder shrank in fear
At rumours that a goat was near.
While all the traders selling food
Close to their wares stood tightly glued,
They didn't track the goat at all,
Which headed for a fabric stall
Where cloth designers' bright creations
Offered succulent temptations:
Mass-produced, or famous name,
Discount – it was all the same –
Billowy blouse or flowery dress:
A banquet for a goat-princess.

The final member of the troupe
Thought he'd like some morning soup,
So with some purpose headed down
In the direction of the town.
On passing by an open door,
An impulse urged him to explore –
But sadly it turned out to be
The central public WC,
Whose clientele all tried to hide
When our marauder peered inside,
Then shrieked, and fled with swift intent,
With many a penny left unspent.
But, praises be, he didn't stay,
But trotted on his merry way
To sample smells, and sounds, and sights,
As shops revealed their rare delights,
And shop assistants raised their eyes
And screamed out loudly in surprise.
Here's a window, take a look,
Maybe I'll devour a book?
Or doubtless I shall find a crop
Of goodies in the Pudding Shop;
Chocolates, souvenirs, antiques –
I haven't had such fun for weeks!

It wasn't until half-past ten
That several teams of burly men
Delivered Bakewell from its plight,
And caught the goats, and roped them tight
Within a pen, and then began
The manhunt for Teetotal Stan.
To tell it shortly, he was found
With empty glass and sorrows drowned,
Then two large constables popped by,
With whom Stan left, with downcast eye,
To spend the rest of market day
Accounting for his goats' affray.
They showed him pictures of the blight
Unleashed on Bakewell, and despite
Regret, repentance and remorse,
The law would duly take its course:
With market mauled, and roses wrecked,
It found Stan guilty of neglect,
And sentenced him to make redress
For all the damage and distress,
An extra order making clear

That should he be discovered near
A goat, or goats, of any sort,
He would be in contempt of court.
A final, helpful hint was made
That Stan might learn the locksmith's trade;
And one last taste of bitter wine
Was that he'd had a parking fine.

Now, many moons since Bakewell's scare,
Calm reigns once more in Rutland Square,
Bath Gardens' blooms are flowering yet,
And safe from cruel, capricious threat;
The tavern has imposed a ban –
For life! – upon Teetotal Stan,
Who in his turn has changed his line,
And taken now to breeding swine.
He likes to hear them snuffle, and squeak…

He's bringing some to town next week.

Bath Gardens (goat-free), Bakewell

23. Annie Ackroyd And The Bottomless Pit

(With due homage to Marriott Edgar, author of "The Lion and Albert", &c)

There once was a Derbyshire couple
From Dove Holes, the Ackroyds by name,
They had a young daughter called Annie,
Who was seven years old, but still tame.

Mrs Ackroyd once fancied an outing,
And her husband said he would come too,
And so did young Annie, their daughter,
'Cos in Dove Holes there's nothing to do.

Mrs Ackroyd said, "Castleton's pretty,
And I'd quite like to visit a cave."
Her husband thought that would be gradely,
And Annie did too, feeling brave.

So they got in the car Sunday morning
And drove off down Castleton way,
They parked a bit outside the village
In a space where you hadn't to pay.

They found their way back through the high street
Past establishments selling Blue John,
Mrs Ackroyd kept scanning the windows
Till her husband said loudly, "Come on!"

They walked up the road past the carpark
With no more delay or ado,
Till they finally reached Speedwell Cavern
And stood at the end of the queue.

Mr Ackroyd remarked, "We've forgotten
To tell our small child what we'll see,
Now Annie dear, if you feel frightened
Just stick by your mother and me.

We're going to go on a boat ride
In a tunnel that won't be well lit,
It starts down some steps underneath us
And ends at the Bottomless Pit.

You might be a touch apprehensive,
'Cos an underground boat's a bit queer,
But to help us remember our outing
You can pick up a nice souvenir."

Well, Annie was somewhat placated,
So wasn't a major concern
As they paid for a family ticket
And patiently waited their turn.

They stood for about half an hour
Until it was their turn to go
Through a door and then down a dark stairway
To an underground jetty below.

They boarded a boat with some others
And soon had set off on their ride,
The Ackroyds both held onto Annie
In case she fell over the side.

The tunnel was quite claustrophobic,
The roof being low and all that,
And the boat was a little too narrow
For anyone bulgy or fat.

They nonetheless made steady progress,
And laughed at the words of the guide
Who cheerily talked about flooding,
Or tourists who'd tragically died.

When they got to the end of the tunnel,
One half of their journey was done,
So they disembarked into a cavern
Which promised additional fun.

The guide pointed out some attractions
Like stalactites, shadows and stuff,
Until Annie, who was only seven
Had, reasonably, heard quite enough.

Now, placed here and there in the cavern
Were artefacts found in the mine,
Including a few leaden beakers
Which Annie thought notably fine.

Recalling the words of her father -
"You can pick up a nice souvenir",
The child, who was quite literal-minded,
Quite quickly conceived an idea.

She stuffed one deep into her pocket,
Which weighed the girl down quite a bit,
Then found, while the guide was still blathering,
She was stood by the Bottomless Pit.

She peered right down into the water,
For the girl was a curious soul,
And, what with the lead being heavy,
She tumbled straight into the hole.

As the splash echoed right round the cavern,
Which splashes in caves tend to do,
The parents strolled up to the poolside,
Where Annie had vanished from view.

The Ackroyds were stumped by the problem,
But wished in no way to lose face,
So called down the hole to their daughter,
But Annie had sunk without trace.

They stood making light conversation
While wondering what to do next,
When the guide, who had finished his lecture,
Came up to them both, looking vexed.

He said, "A lead beaker is missing,
And I fear that your daughter's to blame,
And though I can't prove that she took it,
It's a blot on the day, all the same.

In addition, a dip in the water
Is not technically part of the tour,
So I'm sorry to say, Mrs Ackroyd,
You owe us £11 more."

Mrs Ackroyd observed that, aged seven,
Her Annie was only half-price,
And, since no-one had witnessed the mishap,
An additional charge wasn't nice.

The guide was unwilling to haggle,
Saying that was the usual rate,
But the other folk started to mutter,
And fear that they'd all be back late.

With reluctance the guide dropped the matter
And the tourists got back in the boat,
Which, lacking the Ackroyds' young daughter,
Was just that bit safer to float.

It chugged its way back, minus Annie –
An embarrassing state of affairs,
Till they found themselves back at the entrance
And made their way out up the stairs.

Well, the police came and questioned the Ackroyds,
The interview lasting a while,
When in came a man…bringing Annie! –
Which quite caused her parents to smile.

The policeman was most understanding,
And said he'd no reason to stay,
And though Annie was moister than usual,
He hoped they'd all had a nice day.

When they'd got back to Dove Holes and dried her,
She recounted her tale, bit by bit,
How the weight of the lead dragged her under
And down through the Bottomless Pit.

But then she'd been caught by a current
Which led to an underground stream,
That carried her out of the hillside
Near a van, where she'd had an ice-cream.

They said they'd no reason to doubt her,
And were glad she was back safe and sound,
Though they thought, when they next had an outing,
They'd not go so far underground.

"And it's been a good day, notwithstanding,"
The little child's mother opined,
"That beaker you stuffed in your pocket
Is worth more than tuppence, you'll find."

The final word came from her father,
Whilst grinning from ear to ear,
"You went in that water for nothing,
And came home with a free souvenir!"

Annie's journey into (but not out of) Speedwell Cavern on the outskirts of Castleton can indeed for a modest cost be currently experienced by the speleologically-inclined tourist, following in the (wettish) footsteps of eighteenth-century miners on the lookout for fluorspar. Killjoys will have it that the so-called Bottomless Pit is these days filled nearly up to the top with miners' rubble; but no sensible folk are going to want to test the claim out for themselves, are they; and anyway small girls doubtless have their own ways with Bottomless Pits. They are also inordinately fond of ice cream, so the story must be true…

Gone, But Not Forgotten

24. Brough Stuff

"It's tough at Brough," the soldier said
(Of course he called it Navio,
Named from the rushing river Noe):
"The wind quite hurts my head.
I wish the brass would let me go
Back home to Rome instead."

"But sir," the journalist replied
(He'd come by *cursus publicus* –
An early type of express bus),
"You've got such stunning countryside:
The landscape's simply fabulous –
Just take it in your stride!"

The legionary looked askance
(He'd heard this kind of thing before
From folk beyond Britannia's shore)
And gave the hills a glance.
"If I went rambling on that moor,
I shouldn't stand a chance."

"Indeed?" rejoined the Roman guest
(Who still smelt of the journey's grime,
And fancied it was dinnertime.)
"Perhaps I could suggest –."
The other answered curtly, "I'm –
To cut it short – depressed.

My sword's too old, the water's cold
(And, by the way, you might report
That Brough is *not* a five-star fort);
The bread goes blue with mould.
Those pesky British can't be caught;
It stinks, if truth be told."

He sloped off to a flimsy hut
("Luxurious barracks, hearths aglow,
Never a sight of hail or snow")
And kicked a mangy mutt.
The old reporter watched him go,
And snapped his tablet shut.

Months later, back in Rome, the chill
He'd felt brought forth a thoughtful grunt:
"The truth? Or true-ish? Biased? Blunt?"
He mused, with seasoned skill;
At length he wrote:
              "ALL QUIET – STILL –
UPON THE NORTHERN FRONT".

The Roman fort at Brough (from the Old English burh, *a fortification) guarded a crossing of the River Noe that was probably important for the transportation of lead, mined in the surrounding hills. Tantalising new evidence accumulated by the Wirksworth Roman Project suggests that a hitherto-unknown Roman road led, via Ashford and Robin Hood's Stride, to the lead-mining centre of Wirksworth, which was just conceivably the Roman* Lutudarum. Navio *is quiet and picturesque today, while it's hard to envisage the combination of leaden loads and leaden skies as constituting every Roman soldier's dream posting. Perhaps the local fish tasted nice.*

25. Derwent Drowned

Full threescore years ago, and ten,
A village looked its last
Upon a peaceful past;
And all who dwelt or worshipped here
In ill-starred Derwent, spoke that year
A sad amen.

For dampness came, and probed, and chose
To fill each silent street,
And lapped at laggards' feet,
Until there was no turning back
As, eyeing sacred steeple-stack,
The waters rose,

Then gently crept up ghosts of walls,
As thresholds sank away
Lost from the light of day,
Until the broken hamlet left
The living land, and slept bereft
Of children's calls.

The old church spire pointed on;
While, robbed and wrecked, the nave
Was washed by godless wave,
Until they could not let the tower
Disturb the face of Ladybower…
So all was gone.

And yet, when once as nightbirds cried
I pondered the lagoon
Beneath a midnight moon,
I fancied that I heard a knell,
Knolled by a muffled, mournful bell
That tolled, and sighed.

The demolished remains of the villages of Derwent and Ashopton lie beneath Ladybower Reservoir whose waters began to rise in 1944. Derwent Church tower was initially spared, and persisted rather eerily above the waterline with the intention of being allowed to serve as a memorial, but it was decided to destroy it by dynamite a mere three years later. The church bell was removed and eventually rehung in Chaddesden Church, near Derby, in 1955, although this fact does not, however, stop the wistful-minded from still hearing its spectral chime come stealing across the water when poetic conditions are favourable.

26. Bakewell To Manchester Central, Spring 1963

Standing on the platform aged five-and-a-quarter,
Looking past the sidings where the line curves away,
Mummy checking tickets as I'm patted by a porter,
10.25 and the train's not far away.
Squinting at the signal in the haze of the morning,
(It's bent like a bow although I know it can't be true,)
Watching out for shunting while we wait upon the platform,
Suddenly a bell, and my Mummy says "It's due!"
Gathering the baggage with renewed anticipation,
Looking quite impatient as we never want to wait,
Suddenly it's there and chuffing hard into the station,
"A steamer," Mummy grumbles, "so no wonder it's so late."
I take this to be gospel and we hurry down the carriages,
Hoping to discover a compartment that is free,
Though if we ever found one I don't think that I recall it,
But we sit down all the same and Mummy has a cup of tea.
Faded yellow lights and a strap above the window,
But engine smoke is smutty so we keep the window shut,
Time to look outside as we pass Pineapple Cottages,
Then funny, birdy hawthorns which the local gang have cut.
On through Great Longstone, then dark through Headstone Tunnel,
Sudden rushing echo that a boy wants to pass,
Then out upon the viaduct, and sudden silver brightness,
River, hills and greenery, and smoke past the glass.
Always stop at Miller's Dale (where once I rode my tricycle
Up and down the platform while my father had a fit),
And then round the triangle to Peak Forest quarries,
A landscape of limedust, limestone and grit.
Yet another tunnel onto Chapel and to Chinley:
A bumper-looking station where we always have to wait,
Before we're off again towards Manchester Central…
A journey lost forever after nineteen-sixty-eight.

In the 1960s the old Midland railway line through the Peak District still formed part of a major route from London St Pancras to Manchester that passed in these parts through Matlock, Bakewell and Miller's Dale and in particular over the spectacular Monsal Dale viaduct. The line's closure in 1968 has been seen by many ever since as heartlessly unromantic yet also premature and short-sighted, especially given the ever-increasing road traffic that challenges local planners. Peak Rail *have heroically re-opened the section from Matlock to Rowsley; maybe somehow trains can be restored one day from here to Buxton. In the meantime the route's current incarnation as the Monsal Trail delights walkers and cyclists, although the curious lineside topiary that you once passed a mile before alighting at Bakewell is now just a fading memory.*

Headstone Viaduct, Monsal Dale

67

That Tragic History

27. Sweet Ann Swindel

There dwelt a lass in Ashford Dale,
As sweet a lass as wore a veil,
Or wept by waters clear;
By coolest Wye did she make moan:
"O, must I wander here alone
With ne'er a leman dear?"

While thus she cried "Alas, the day",
There rode young John along her way,
Fast by that reedy brake,
And there did stop, and there espied
That fair upon the water's side,
And made him bold to speak:

"I am John Eyre of Bakewell town,
It grieves my heart to see thy frown,
Pray, what doth ail thee so?"
"O, sir, my mother is no more,
My father's heart is struck full sore,
And leman have I no."

"O fairest Ann, wilt thou be mine?
Thy rosy lips and starry eyne
Do stir my love for thee!"
"Upon these banks of rippling Wye,
Sweet John, I swear, else may I die,
Thy truelove shall I be."

"Then hie thee hence to Bakewell town,
Where thou shalt buy thy bridal gown,
And wed we twain shall be;
Come, weep not at the water's side,
For thou shalt be a soldier's bride.
And from thy burthens free."

So fared sweet Ann to Bakewell town,
Where she did buy her bridal gown,
But John, he came not nigh.
"O, good King George hath ta'en him far
Across the seas to fight his war –
Methinks he's like to die."

Then sweet Ann Swindel wept full sore,
To Ashford green her steps she bore,
Where flows the stream full nigh;
As near Wye's flood her tears did spill,
She fainted by the whisp'ring rill,
And breathed her latest sigh.

The wars did cease ere they begun,
Brave John to Bakewell town did run
Sweet Ann his bride to make;
"O, seek not thou thy blooming bride –
By Ashford's stream her soul doth bide;
For thee her heart did break."

The passing bell for Ann did sound,
They bore her corse to holy ground,
And set her garland high
That all who see it might bewail
The lot of sweet Ann of the dale,
Who yet a maid did die.

In some places it was the custom in days gone by, should a village girl die young and unmarried, to carry in her funeral procession a maiden garland, or crants, which would afterwards be left in the church. Five such fragile paper garlands survive in Holy Trinity Church, Ashford-in-the-Water, one of which was in memory of a local girl, Ann Swindel, who died unwed in 1798, aged just 22. She is buried in the churchyard, but the inscription on her weathered gravestone can no longer be read. The cause of her death is unknown, so in my poem I have suggested a reason – akin to that adduced in Hamlet *for Ophelia, who was also 'allow'd her virgin crants' (V i 240).*

28. William Mompesson's Lament

When late abed I'm lying
In the throes of fitful dream,
I feel again the anguish
Since I came to serve at Eyam.

I still see Mary Cooper
Holding poor George Viccars' cloth;
I see her son fast fading –
Why did *they* deserve God's wrath?

I watch the Bradshaws fleeing
The Dark Angel's pinching grip,
Then glimpse a mourner's teardrop,
Or a stoic's quiv'ring lip.

When ousted Thomas Stanley
First responded to my plea,
And jointly we petitioned all
The townsfolk not to flee,

I felt within my deepest soul
My deepest-ever dread
That hectored then and tortures now:
A corpse within my bed.

O, where are now the Talbots?
They sleep at Riley's farm;
And where the heart-walled Hancocks,
Seven souls whom none can harm?

O, where my dearest Katherine
Who thought the air so sweet?
I see a crown of righteousness
That hovers at my feet.

O, where more than two hundred souls,
Unselfish martyrs all?
Each still lies wrapped, beside me,
In an otherworldly pall.

"A plague on both your houses!"
Cried the doomed Mercutio;
A plague on *all* our houses
Was Eyam's doom.

The rest you know.

In September 1665 a parcel of cloth samples from plague-ridden London was delivered to a tailor, George Viccars, who was lodging with Eyam resident Mary Cooper. A few days later he and one of Mary's sons had succumbed to the infamously deadly disease, which thereafter began taking its dreadful toll upon the village. Some families such as the wealthy Bradshaws had taken the opportunity to leave before the rector, William Mompesson, and his Puritan predecessor Thomas Stanley whom he had replaced come the Restoration jointly persuaded the rest of the inhabitants to remain in the village so that the infection did not spread. Almost all did; but by the end of the plague's visitation fourteen months later 260 parishioners had died, including seven members each of the Talbot and Hancock families, the latter lying ever since within a heart-shaped wall in a field just outside the village – the Riley Graves. Mompesson survived, but his wife Katherine had one day remarked that the air seemed to smell particularly sweet: this was, however, an all-too-ominous sign that the plague had finally caught up with her, and she duly became its 200th victim.
A yearly service is held on the last Sunday in August in Cucklet Delph to commemorate the heroic villagers whose lives were cut short by 'The Plague of Eyam'.

29. Cressbrook Mill – Then

"One winter's day, at eight years old,
I came to Cressbrook Mill,
The snow was falling, and I felt
The cold wind's bitter chill.

I touched a piece of paper
With a scarlet seal thereon,
Which bound me as a 'prentice
Till the age of twenty-one.

They put me onto carding,
Hard by a drawing-frame,
And there I worked from 5 a.m.
Until the night-time came.

Rising without breaking fast
We laboured through the day,
And snatched brief meals of oatcake
Or porridge thin and grey.

We feared the master-carder,
The evil Thomas Birks:
As Tom-the-Devil he was known,
And did the Devil's works.

He'd throw the girls across his knee
Afore the men and boys,
And flog them till all hands were shocked
But dared not make a noise.

One day a boy who worked with me
Did make our frame to break,
I said 'twas I that did it,
But that was a mistake:

The overlooker beat me
With a stick about my head,
So savagely and sorely, it
Was full of lumps, and bled.

A woman, Sarah Goodling,
Fell lingeringly sick,
She stopped her frame, so Tom-the-Devil
Felled her with his stick.

Three times she rose with slipping grip,
Three times Tom beat her down,
Until she lay upon the floor,
With blood upon her gown.

They bore poor Sarah up the stairs,
And laid her on her bed,
With herbal tea to soothe her, but
By nightfall she was dead.

Another, Betsy Witnough,
Had bad bread in her bowl,
So crept into the little-house
And threw it down the hole.

This angered Mrs Newton,
The mistress at that time,
Who said she'd shave the heads of all
Who covered up the crime.

A frightened girl called Caroline
Said Betsy'd thrown the bread;
The master beat brave Betsy blind
Then flung her on her bed.

Poor Betsy ailed, poor Betsy starved,
And thirsted till she cried,
One night she stole out to the pond,
Wherein she slipped, and died.

Ten years I toiled at Cressbrook Mill,
And fretted with much dread,
Quite sovereign-yellow was my skin,
Quite dateless was my head.

At last my brother saw his chance
And stole me thence away;
But witless and half-doited
I remain unto this day."

30. Cressbrook Mill – Now

The sunset shades envelop Cressbrook Mill,
The day's great eye descends behind the hill,
The river's pool lies tranquil, trickling still.

Apartments now, of a superior kind,
The mill-house rears, untroubled and refined,
Where modern bourgeois watch the river wind.

Does any feel its history? Who knows
What dreams died in this dale, or might suppose
That fear once flourished here, where twilight glows?

Does one suspect, snug in a favourite chair,
That once, within that cubic yard of air
A 'prentice-girl bewailed her shaven hair;

Or, starving cold upon a fleck-strewn floor
A weaver-boy collapsed to rise no more,
Where now fridge-magnets clothe the freezer door?

The atrocious treatment of young boy and girl apprentices at mills like Cressbrook during the nineteenth century was not merely a little local difficulty: it was a particularly nasty blot on the national escutcheon. It is hard now to envisage such a tranquil corner of one of the most beautiful dales in England as a living hell, but such it was for many a young victim. The names in Cressbrook Mill – Then *are all of real people, and the poem draws on their own testimony, which was recorded in* The Ashton Chronicle *in 1849. Slowly, conditions in such places improved as a result of public pressure, but how many young lives were ruined along the way will never be known.*

Rocks, and Stones, and Trees

31. The Roaches

By ribboned road the Roaches rise –
A wizard's world of sky and stone;
Alone in silent land they loom
Save for the crows' cacophonous cries.

Once, shaped by shows of chivalry
Sir Gawain braved the Green Knight's boast:
Was this the spot the swordsman sought
Upon his day of destiny?

Was Lud's cool Church the chapel green
Where Gawain feared he'd forfeit all
By single stroke from elfin axe –
A curious quest for King and Queen?

Lost, latterly, in troubled time
Dissenters dared to hurry here,
(No friends of an official faith)
In spite of snow, or rain, or rime.

Now, strange, high home to flower and fern
In solitude these rocks still rear,
Where winds wrap tight 'round whin and tree,
And folklore's flickering embers burn.

The Roaches comprise a gritstone ridge lying in wild countryside between Buxton and Leek. Secreted within the rocks is a cleft known as Lud's Church, which some have suggested is the original Green Chapel featured in the medieval alliterative poem Sir Gawain and the Green Knight, whither the Arthurian champion rides to a fearful rendezvous with his weird, otherworldly opponent, thinking that he's due to be beheaded. The concealed spot is also thought to have served as a meeting place for the 14th century Lollards, dissenting followers of John Wycliffe. It's an eerie place, full of fantasy and shadows of the past.

32. A Dry Stone Waller

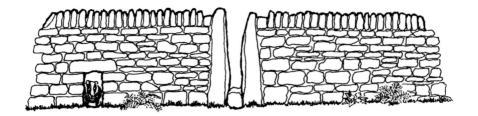

They call him Stonewall Jackson of the Dales,
His features fashioned from the very rock,
A landsman lashed for years by rainy gales
Undaunted in his scanty shepherd's smock,

Of sullen speech, of mood expressionless;
Yet there is witchcraft in his ancient hands
Which stroke rude stones, and soothe their edginess
As slowly they succumb to soft commands.

Stone by rising stone, and yard by yard
A shapely wall strides off across the moor,
The craftsman's magic stamp on every shard
That shimmers, mortarless and yet secure.

No plaque his boundary bears, no flattering rhyme,
But Stonewall's monuments will outlast time.

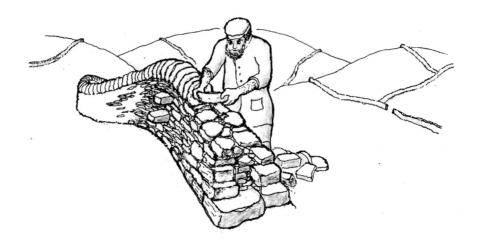

33. Hermitage

Within the womb of Cratcliffe Tor
I keep my bed;
A makeshift pillow stuffed with straw
Receives my head.
Sequestered from the world's keen strife,
I drag the pensive hermit's life.

A beetling hillside, stark and steep
Attends the cell
Wherein I ask that God might keep
Your soul from hell,
And bless the folk who pant their way
To my abode, to watch me pray.

At lonely noon when time runs slow,
I contemplate
The wisps of world that trot below
On Derby Gate,
Whilst one stray shaft of sunlight licks
The shadows off my crucifix,

And fancy that I hear a horn
Upon the breeze
From old Mock Beggars Hall, forlorn
Beyond the trees,
As Robin Hood, with giant stride,
Halloos his outlaws far and wide.

But when the mists mix with the dew
On dripping days,
And dawn dissolves the yearning yew
Beyond my gaze,
I skulk behind imagined bars,
And speed my prayers to unseen stars.

It seems that from time to time in bygone days there really was a hermit occupying the cave at Cratcliffe Tor, near Birchover, since Haddon Hall documents record a payment to "Ye harmitt" in 1549 for supplying the kitchen with ten rabbits. A crucifix carved on the cave wall is perhaps 600 years old. Below the steep rise runs the ancient trackway Derby Gate (from Old Norse gata, *meaning a road), otherwise known as The Portway and now thought to be Roman; and beyond is the rocky outcrop of Robin Hood's Stride, its name a fanciful interpretation of the two highest clumps of rock which lie a few yards apart. These also do duty as the "chimneys" of Mock Beggars Hall, the rock's alternative name: one imagines a starving and maybe slightly credulous wayfarer thinking that he had at last lighted upon an outpost of civilisation only to be confounded by a cruelly mocking and barren Hardyesque landscape. One way or another, there's a lot of recreational climbing to be had in these parts.*

Mock Beggars Hall

80

Ducal Dwellings

Chatsworth House

Haddon Hall, painted by F. W. Botham after an 1850 engraving by T. A. Prior.

34. Palace Of The Peak

Speed me, swift winds, to Chatsworth's tranquil park
So may I feast there in Arcadia!
For when the keen-eyed Duke of olden day
Envisioned how fair fountains high might play
He dreamt a dream to dazzle every soaring lark.

And what a trove is here!
As Talman, Archer brought the wish
Of visionary Cavendish
To rich reality, the house became
A seat for templed craftsmen and their fame,

Whose art commands our eye:
A mythic ceiling by Laguerre,
Or iron-balustraded stair
Where Tijou toiled; or Cupid's curls
Above, or Watson's limewood whorls.

And if, cool breath, you waft me to some tree,
It should not be mere fancy if I feel
Beneath the gaze of Bess's Hunting Tower,
In quiet sojourn by Queen Mary's Bower
An echo of Elysian immortality.

Chatsworth House as it exists today is essentially the vision of William, Duke of Cavendish (1641-1707) and his descendents. William Talman (1650-1719) designed the current South and East fronts, the other two sides probably being the work of Thomas Archer (1668-1743). The Paris Academy-trained Louis Laguerre (1663-1721) painted many of the classically-themed ceilings, and the Huguenot Jean Tijou (fl. c1690-1710) created some significant ironwork. Samuel Watson of Heanor (1662-1715) was chief woodcarver. The Hunting Tower of 1581 is named after Derbyshire's formidable matriarch Elizabeth 'Bess' of Hardwick (1520-1608) who became Countess of Shrewsbury; and Queen Mary's Bower was reputedly where Mary, Queen of Scots (1542-87) once rested whilst on her unwilling perigrinations from one English country house to another. No wonder Jane Austen (1775-1817) used Chatsworth as the model for Pemberley in Pride and Prejudice *(1797-1813).*

35. Xanadu For Dorothy

*("In Xanadu did Kubla Khan
A stately pleasure-dome decree....")*

By Haddon Fields did Vernon seed
A stately manor house decree,
Where Wye, the rippling river, flowed
Through meadows, where gilt kingcups glowed
And lit each willow tree.

And so the Hall, on fertile ground
With battlements was girdled round.
And here were gardens, more than passing fair,
Where flourished many a bloom of damasked rose,
And here was woodland, ancient as the air,
Enfolding every greenery that grows.

And oh! The old romantic tale that chants
To every beating heart that ever leapt:
A secret flight! No cries of uncles, aunts
Could stifle a young maiden's sigh, that haunts
The stair whence to a lovers' tryst she crept.

At Haddon Hall the past reposes,
Mid the trees and scented roses.
Linger once, and twice, and thrice,
And close your eyes, let cares recede,
'For here on honey-dew we feed,
And drink the milk of Paradise.'

(After "Kubla Khan" by Samuel Taylor Coleridge)

The Vernon family acquired the manor of Haddon in 1170 and were responsible for building most of the medieval Hall that survives today. Legend has it that, in 1563, the young Dorothy Vernon managed to elope during a ball and meet her waiting lover John Manners (of whom Dorothy's father disapproved); the couple then rode away to be married. Opinion is divided as to the truth of the tale, but it contains enough romantic relish to have inspired stories, plays, a film and Sir Arthur Sullivan's light opera Haddon Hall.

A Peakland Pot-Pourri

36. A Light Bite In Longnor

What do you do with an old market hall -
Where a century ago each fourpenny stall
Could be six foot in length, and not an inch more,
Where "cheese, ducks or poultry not in baskets, per score"
Attracted a levy of tuppence when sold,
The same as on bulls bought at two years old?

You make it a venue for locals to dance in –
Then nowadays, if you should happen to glance in
You'll find there a sanctum for coffee, and crafts,
Within the old walls that still keep out the drafts,
Where time seems to crawl in an old-fashioned way,
And Abbie's fresh ginger cake begs you to stay.

So if showers make cobblestones glisten and gleam,
There's always a scone…and another; with cream…

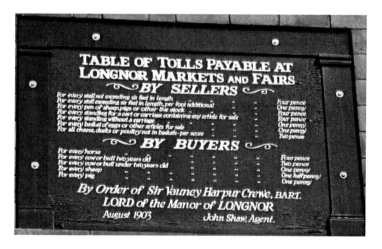

The Market Hall in Longnor, Staffordshire dates from 1873, and like many buildings of its type saw various uses before its current incarnation as a coffee and crafts centre. Although Longnor would nowadays probably come under the "sleepy village" category it was in days of yore a relatively important settlement within an otherwise sparsely-populated landscape. Local Lord of the Manor Sir Vauncy Harper Crewe was an eccentric recluse who lived in a kind of time warp at Calke Abbey where he spent most of his days shooting the birds on his estate. He also owned tracts of moorland around Longnor where he spent any time left over walking and, er, shooting. A rare example of an aristocratic taxidermist, Sir Vauncy evidently enjoyed knocking the stuffing out of anything with a pair of wings…and then cramming it all back in again. For the curious, the results of his extensive labours are still on (rather dimly-lit) display at Calke Abbey, some ten miles south of Derby.

37. A Smug Hen's Rhyme At Roosting Time

At New House Farm there grows a tree,
With boughs so strong and sturdy
That it can bear the likes of me –
A comfort-loving birdie.
When evening shades bring calm to croft,
And sleep to farmyard fauna,
On stumpy wings I soar aloft,
And choose a snoozeful corner.

From here, before the land of Nod
Engulfs my every feather,
I scrutinise each stone and sod,
And hope for decent weather.
My vantage-point affords a view
Denied to goose or gander,
Until black night hides lamb and ewe
And shrouds my snug veranda.

Beyond the reach of midnight clocks
I dream of corn eternal,
Until the wretched farmyard cocks
Commence their din infernal:
Their clarion cock-a-doodle-doo
Resounds at half past four:
It wakes the dead in Timbuktu,
And deafens millions more.

But now's the hour that tragedy
Can stalk a cocksure fowl,
When Kniveton's impious Mr Todd
Resumes his lethal prowl:
Too soon a cock will brave the dawn –
Too slow and… ah, too late!
While wise old hens are left to mourn
His cruel, unfeathered fate.

*

New House Farm near Kniveton is not only home to smug hens and reckless cockerels but also plays year-round host to a steady trickle of WWOOFers – folk availing themselves of World-Wide Opportunities on Organic Farms. For more information, visit www.newhousefarm.co.uk.

38. Butterfly At Bradwell

March day, cold clay, sun weakly weaving,
Chill air, threadbare the ground, still grieving;
Dark form, wings warm, to worn wall cleaving:
                    Small Tortoiseshell!

Last year, sky clear, when first it fluttered,
Abloom with broom the fields were buttered;
Before the craw of autumn spluttered
                    It battened well.

Late fall, when squall blew helter-skelter,
In hole or bole it sought safe shelter,
To sit, unlit, a dark, dry Delta
                    While weeds lay dead.

Reborn, this dawn, by wheeled world beckoned,
Sleep shed, sun-led each febrile second
It's there on bare, bright brick, with fecund
                    Fortune ahead.

Time's token, woken wings aquiver,
Evades dank shades with shrug and shiver
As, dight with light, a young beam-giver
                    Strives, strains to see

Four freckled, speckled petals, hailing
A flash of brashly scarlet scaling,
Lift, soft, aloft on breezes sailing:
                    Spring's sky-jewel. Free.

39. Fidelis In Omnibus*

Hurrah for Henry Hulley!
Who in 1921
Bought the first of many buses
Which have run and run and run:
He started with a famous Ford,
The modern Model T,
And ever since his name's been part
Of Peak mythology.

From Baslow buses spread their wings:
To Bakewell first they came,
And Chesterfield, then Youlgrave
Now embraced the Hulley name,
Then onward onto Calver,
To Eyam and Tideswell too,
So village folk could shop, or keep
A secret rendezvous...

Grumbling up a twisty hill,
Or swooshing down a dale,
Hulley's buses weather it
Through rain, and fog, and gale.
If things are rough round Calver Sough
A Hulley's bus won't stall,
For kids don't want to miss a day
Of schooling, after all…

Stranded in a snowdrift?
We'll dig us out – don't fret!
We've done this kind of thing before –
You'll get to Youlgrave yet.
Through slushy streets in younger days
What great relief to greet
Familiar PET 100,
The darling of the fleet.

The odd unscheduled extra stop
To pick up someone's friend,
Bingo-players' gossip
That appeared to have no end:
Happy Hulley memories –
But there'll be many more,
For still his buses ply our lanes,
And drop me at my door.

Trustworthy in everything

Envoi

40. An Exhortation

Come one, come all, attend my call:
To Peakland let us hie,
Forsake the dun and dusty town,
And climb the hillside's towering crown
Enthroned against the sky:
Leave smoky streets for green retreats
Where babbling streamlets play,
In frith or dell let us abide,
Till shadows creep at eventide
To close a sunlit day!

We'll tell a tale of bosky dale
Beloved of hip and haw,
Through waters pure the fishes glide,
Beneath the sheer, precipitous side
Of shiny crag or tor –
Where valley yields to windy fields
An ancient oak broods on,
A witness dumb to many an age
When Nature's penned on Peakland's page
A thrill for everyone!

Upon his lowering low
The curlew opes a plaintive throat,
While in her cave below
A flittermouse squeaks her piping note;
In a flash the merlin flies,
O'er heath'ry moor a-raiding;
The lark ascends the skies
And sends his song cascading!

The sweetest buds of spring
Betoken summer's leafy stands,
Then gusts of autumn bring
Cold winter's bony-fingered hands
That freeze in icy chill,
As storms lash holt and hill,
Till April again once more
Unlocks her Peakland store!

So let us stride where moorland wide
Embraces upland air,
Where Kinder looms, and buttercup blooms,
Where edge and clough meet gorge and grough
And stony outcrops stare:
A gladsome world where cares are hurled
And flung on winds that fly;
A realm that lifts each aching frown:
Come, all, forsake the dusty town –
To Peakland we must hie!

Kinder Scout

A Peakland Suite

WATERS OF THE PEAK

Words and music by Simon Mold

I love these Peak-land streams that flow In peb-bly bed or ver-dant vale,_ Where drifts of wa-ter a-vens blow, And dip-pers dive in Long-den-dale: By_ tin-kling weir_____ and time-less mill,_

winds_____ a - way__ be- low__ To tease the tide___ of rip - - pling

A tempo

Noe.

In Wye's wide meads_____ I'd spend my days____ And gaze on Mon -

- sal Head a-bove, By Lath-kill's lim - pid rill I'd laze,__ Or tread the stones o'er

tum - bling Dove,_ While tawn-y trout flash by my feet. To make_

an ang -ler's day "com- pleat".

But where I crave the no-blest scene The state-ly Der - went slips_in style

From La - dy-bow-er's lake - land sheen To Chats-worth's grand pal - a - tial pile:

Sweet wa-ters! Runes____ in____ Na - tures' rhyme,

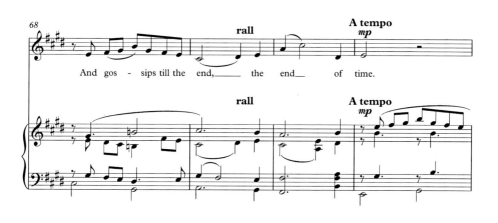

And gos - sips till the end,____ the end____ of time.

4'09.9"

Ann Swindel died unwed in 1798, aged 22. Her maiden garland, or 'crants', still hangs in the church at Ashford-in-the-Water, near Bakewell, Derbyshire.

SWEET ANN SWINDEL

Words and Music by Simon Mold

There dwelt a lass in Ash-ford Dale, As

sweet a lass as wore a veil, Or wept by wa – ters clear; By

coo-lest Wye did_ she make_moan: "O, must I wan - der e'er a-lone With

ne'er my le - man dear?"

"Say,_ swee-test Ann, what ai-leth thee, That

lot of sweet Ann of the dale Who yet a maid did die.

AN EXHORTATION

Simon Mold

Simon Mold

Come one, come all, at - tend my call: To_ Peak-land let us

tell a tale of bos - ky dale Be - loved of hip and

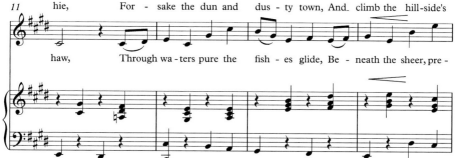

hie, For - sake the dun and dus - ty town, And_ climb the hill-side's

haw, Through wa - ters pure the fish - es glide, Be - neath the sheer, pre -

103

2

cares are hurled And flung on winds that fly; A realm that lifts each

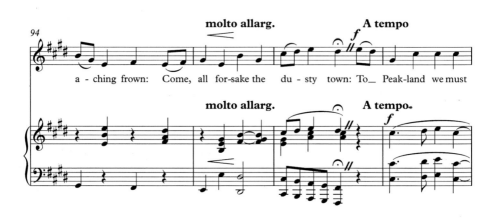

a - ching frown: Come, all for-sake the du - sty town: To Peak-land we must

hie!

17-01-2004/15-03-2016